JUPITER

EARLY BIRD
ASTRONOMY

BY ROSANNA HANSEN

LERNER PUBLICATIONS COMPANY · MINNEAPOLIS

For Kaylie and Finn, two shining stars in my universe

The images in this book are used with the permission of: NASA/JPL, pp. 4, 14, 19, 20, 28, 30, 31, 32 (both), 34 (both), 37, 41 (inset), 48 (both); © Space Frontiers/Taxi/Getty Images, p. 5; © Hulton Archive/Getty Images, pp. 6, 8; © TED ALJIBE/AFP/Getty Images, p. 7; The Granger Collection, New York, p. 9; AP Photo/The Columbus Dispatch, James D. DeCamp, p. 10; NASA, pp. 11, 26; © Laura Westlund/Independent Picture Service, pp. 12-13, 17, 18, 27; © Antonio M. Rosario/Photographer's Choice/Getty Images, p. 15; The International Astronomical Union/Martin Kornmesser, p. 16; © StockTrek/Photodisc/Getty Images, pp. 21, 39; © Ron Miller, p. 22; M. Wong and I. de Pater (University of California, Berkeley), p. 23; © Jafaris Mustafa/Dreamstime.com, p. 24; © Marta Johnson, p. 25; NASA/John Hopkins University Applied Physics Laboratory/Southwest Research Institute, p. 29; NASA/HQ/GRIN, pp. 33 (left), 36; © Photodisc/Getty Images, p. 33 (right); © Roger Ressmeyer/CORBIS, p. 35; © Time Life Pictures/NASA/Getty Images, pp. 38, 42; © Michael Benson/Kinetikon Pictures/CORBIS, p. 40; © Space Frontiers/Hulton Archive/Getty Images, p. 41 (main); © Charlotte Nation/Riser/Getty Images, p. 43; © Denis Scott/CORBIS, p. 46; © Alan Williams/Alamy, p. 47.

Front cover: © Antonio M. Rosario/Iconica/Getty Images.
Back cover: NASA, ESA, and The Hubble Heritage Team (STScI/AURA).

Lerner Publications Company
A division of Lerner Publishing Group, Inc.
241 First Avenue North
Minneapolis, MN 55401 U.S.A.

Website address: www.lernerbooks.com

Library of Congress Cataloging-in-Publication Data

Hansen, Rosanna.
    Jupiter / by Rosanna Hansen.
        p.   cm. — (Early bird astronomy)
    Includes index.
    ISBN 978–0–7613–4153–6 (lib. bdg. : alk. paper)
    1. Jupiter (Planet)—Juvenile literature. I. Title.
QB661.H365 2010
523.45—dc22   2008045440

Manufactured in the United States of America
1 2 3 4 5 6 – BP – 15 14 13 12 11 10

CONTENTS

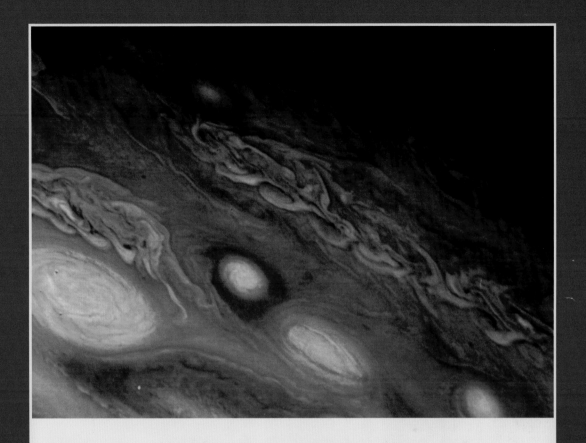

BE A WORD DETECTIVE

Can you find these words as you read about Jupiter? Be a detective and try to figure out what they mean. You can turn to the glossary on page 46 for help.

astronomer	gas giant	spacecraft
atmosphere	orbit	telescope
axis	rotate	
crater	solar system	

This statue shows the Roman god Jupiter. Why is the planet Jupiter named for this god?

CHAPTER 1
KING OF THE PLANETS

Jupiter is often called the king of the planets. It is the biggest planet. All the other planets could easily fit inside Jupiter. It has the name of a king too. The Romans gave Jupiter its name long ago. The Romans believed in many gods. They named Jupiter after the king of their gods.

Jupiter can often be seen in the night sky. When it appears, it shines with a creamy white glow. Jupiter is one of the brightest objects we can see. Only three objects are brighter than Jupiter. These three are the Sun, our Moon, and the planet Venus.

The planets **Venus** (TOP LEFT) **and Jupiter** (TOP RIGHT) **and a crescent Moon** (BELOW) **were seen unusually close together in the night sky in December 2008.**

People have watched Jupiter for thousands of years. Four hundred years ago, a scientist named Galileo studied Jupiter. At first, he watched this planet using only his eyes. People had always watched Jupiter that way. Then Galileo learned about the telescope (TEH-luh-skohp). It was a new invention at that time. It made distant things look closer. Galileo wanted to see Jupiter more closely. So he built his own small telescope.

Galileo made important discoveries about Jupiter using his telescope.

Galileo kept track of the objects around Jupiter over several days. He made this drawing to show how they moved. The circle stands for Jupiter.

Galileo used his homemade telescope to watch Jupiter. Soon he saw something amazing. Four objects were traveling around Jupiter. They were moons! Galileo was the first person to see these moons. Before that, people only knew about Earth's Moon.

Modern scientists use big, powerful telescopes to study Jupiter. Scientists have also sent several spacecraft close to Jupiter. A spacecraft is a vehicle that travels in space. These spacecraft have taken many photos of Jupiter. The photos show us how Jupiter looks up close.

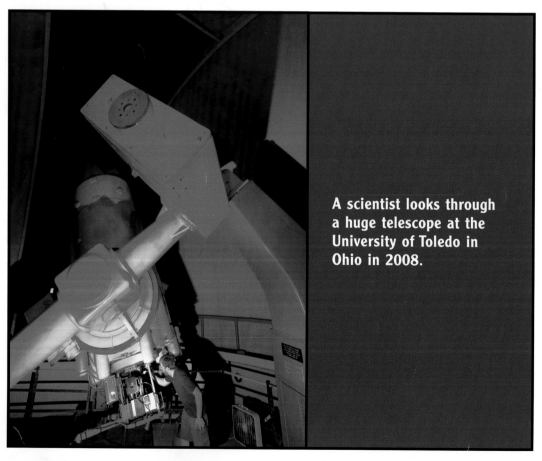

A scientist looks through a huge telescope at the University of Toledo in Ohio in 2008.

Clouds make up Jupiter's colorful stripes.

Jupiter is a colorful planet. It is covered with orange, red, white, and brown stripes. These stripes are really frozen clouds.

Underneath its icy clouds, Jupiter is made of gases. This planet does not have a solid surface. You could not stand or walk on Jupiter. Instead, you would sink deeper and deeper inside the planet!

Neptune

Pluto

Uranus

Saturn

Jupiter

CHAPTER 2
THE FIFTH PLANET FROM THE SUN

Jupiter and Earth share the same neighborhood in space. They are both part of the solar system. The solar system includes the Sun and eight planets. It has dwarf planets too. These are smaller than the eight main planets. Rocky objects called asteroids and comets are also part of the solar system.

12

This diagram shows planets and objects in our solar system. The asteroid belt and Kuiper belt are groups of rocky and icy objects.

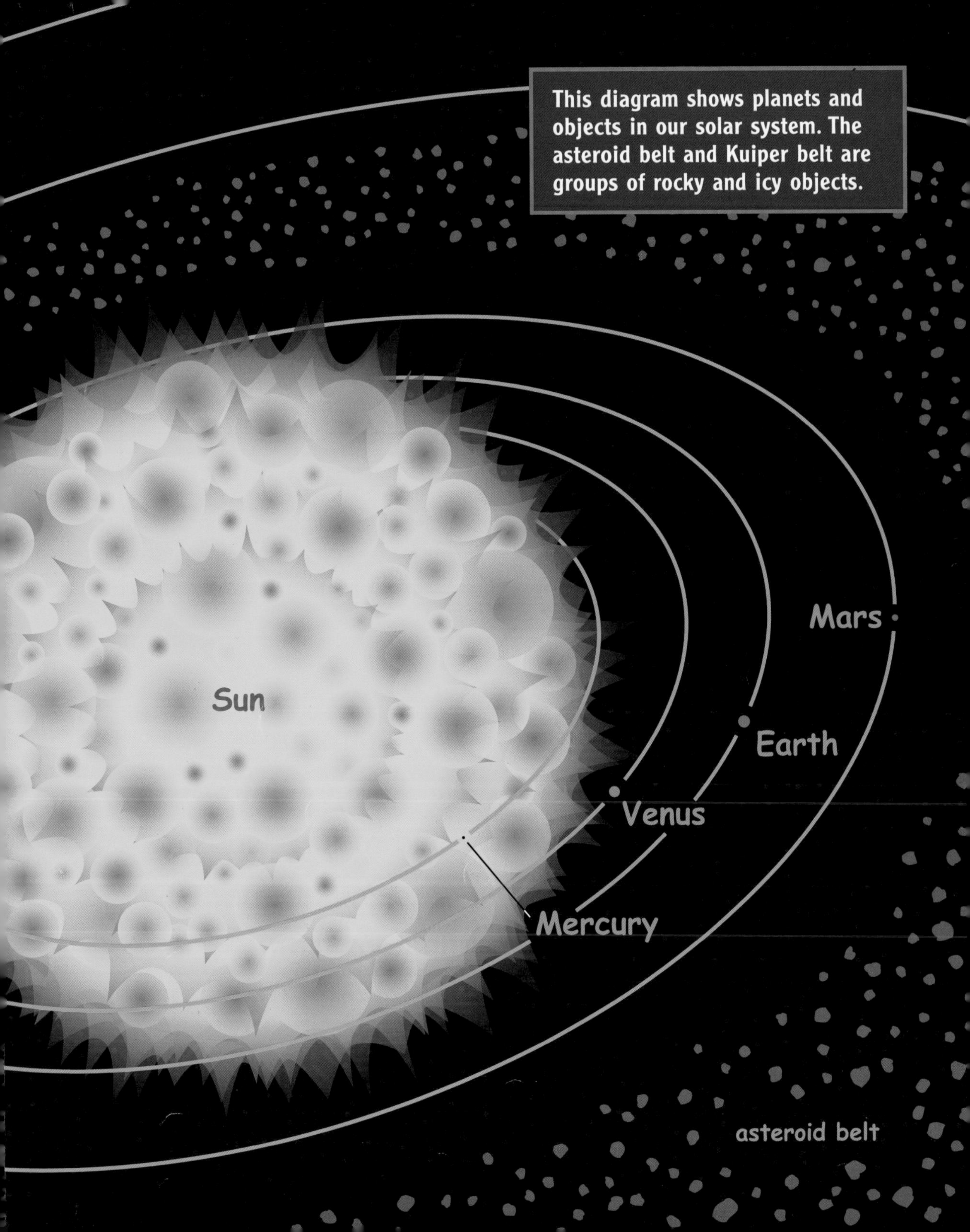

Mars

Earth

Sun

Venus

Mercury

asteroid belt

The surface of Mars is rocky. The four planets closest to the Sun are made of rock.

The Sun lies at the center of the solar system. The planets closest to the Sun are Mercury, Venus, Earth, and Mars. These four planets are mostly made of solid rock. Scientists call them the rocky planets. Jupiter, Saturn, Uranus, and Neptune are called gas giants. They are mostly made of gas. They are the largest planets in the solar system and the farthest from Earth.

Jupiter is the fifth planet from the Sun. It is about 484 million miles (778 million kilometers) away from the Sun. That is about five times farther from the Sun than Earth is.

This illustration shows the Sun as it would look from just beyond Jupiter.

Jupiter is much bigger than the other planets. If you could draw a line through the middle of Jupiter, it would be 88,846 miles (142,984 km) long. Eleven Earths would fit along that line! And if Jupiter were empty, more than 1,300 Earths could fit inside it. It is huge!

This picture shows the eight planets in our solar system. The Sun appears on the left, and the dwarf planet Pluto is on the right. This picture shows the size of each planet compared to others.

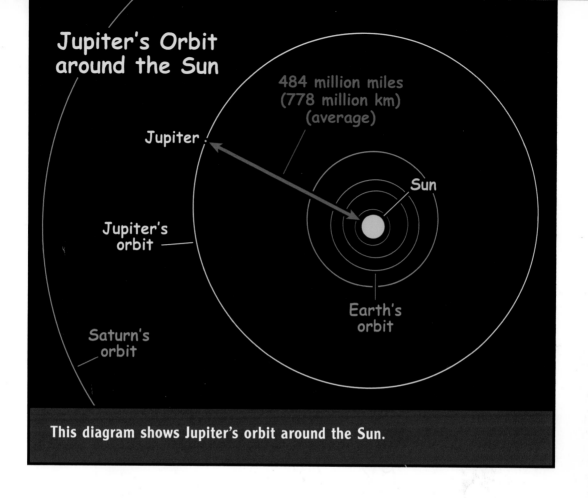

Jupiter's Orbit
around the Sun

484 million miles
(778 million km)
(average)

Jupiter

Sun

Jupiter's
orbit

Earth's
orbit

Saturn's
orbit

This diagram shows Jupiter's orbit around the Sun.

All the planets travel in a curved path around the Sun. Each planet's path is called its orbit.

Earth orbits the Sun in one year. But Jupiter's orbit is much larger than Earth's. Jupiter takes almost 12 Earth years to orbit the Sun one time.

Each planet also spins around its axis
(AK-sis). An axis is an imaginary line through
the center of a planet. When a planet spins
this way, we say that it rotates (ROH-tayts).
Some of the planets rotate quickly. Others
rotate more slowly.

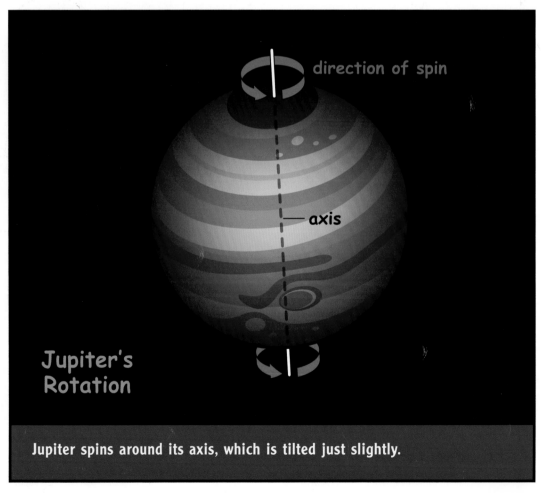

direction of spin

axis

Jupiter's
Rotation

Jupiter spins around its axis, which is tilted just slightly.

These pictures were taken as Jupiter rotated. It made one full rotation between the third picture (TOP RIGHT) and the last (BOTTOM RIGHT). You can see Jupiter's dark spot in the same position (LOWER LEFT OF THE PLANET) in both photos.

The time it takes a planet to rotate once equals one day on that planet. Earth spins around once every 24 hours. Jupiter rotates much faster than Earth. In fact, this planet rotates faster than any other planet. It spins around once every 9 hours and 55 minutes. So one day on Jupiter is less than 10 hours!

Jupiter's colorful clouds surround the planet. What makes up these clouds?

CHAPTER 3

JUPITER CLOSE-UP

The planet Jupiter has a thick layer of clouds around it. These clouds are the top of Jupiter's atmosphere (AT-muhs-feer). An atmosphere is the blanket of gases around a planet. Most of Jupiter's highest clouds are made of the gas ammonia. Scientists think some of the lower clouds contain ice or water.

Jupiter's clouds form colorful stripes. The dark stripes are called belts. They are orange, brown, or red. The light stripes are called zones. The zones are white, yellow, or tan in color. Sometimes the zones also have little patches of blue.

This image of Jupiter shows the planet's orange, brown, and red belts, as well as white, yellow, and tan zones.

This illustration shows the storms and lightning in Jupiter's atmosphere.

Wind creates the zones and belts on Jupiter.
Strong winds blow across this giant planet.
These winds push the clouds around and
around Jupiter, creating stripes.

The winds make Jupiter a stormy planet
too. Its clouds are full of storms and lightning.
The clouds swirl and change shape all the time.
Some clouds change very quickly. Other clouds
take hundreds of years to change.

The Great Red Spot is one of the largest storms on Jupiter. This storm has raged for more than three hundred years. It is shaped like a huge oval. Two planets as big as Earth could fit inside the Great Red Spot!

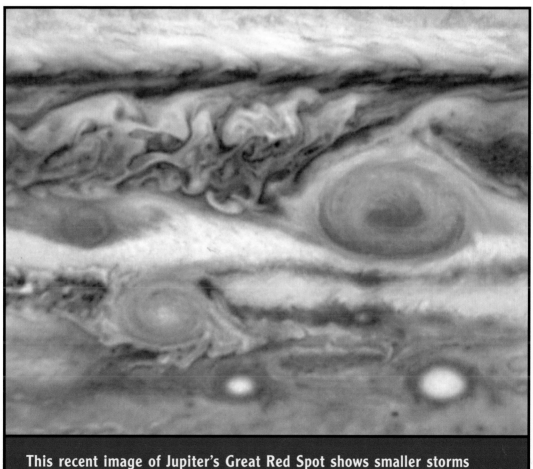

This recent image of Jupiter's Great Red Spot shows smaller storms around it.

Below Jupiter's layer of clouds, the atmosphere is made of two gases. These gases are hydrogen (HY-druh-jehn) and helium (HEE-lee-uhm). Most of Jupiter is hydrogen gas, with some helium mixed in.

These balloons float in the air because they are filled with helium. Jupiter's atmosphere has helium in it, along with hydrogren.

Water and steam are made of hydrogen and oxygen. Hydrogen gas and liquid make up most of Jupiter.

Deep inside Jupiter, the hydrogen changes from a gas to a liquid. This is because of pressure from Jupiter's atmosphere. This pressure squeezes the hydrogen gas tightly together. When hydrogen gas is squeezed tightly enough, it becomes a liquid. Deeper down, the liquid hydrogen changes again. It becomes a liquid metal.

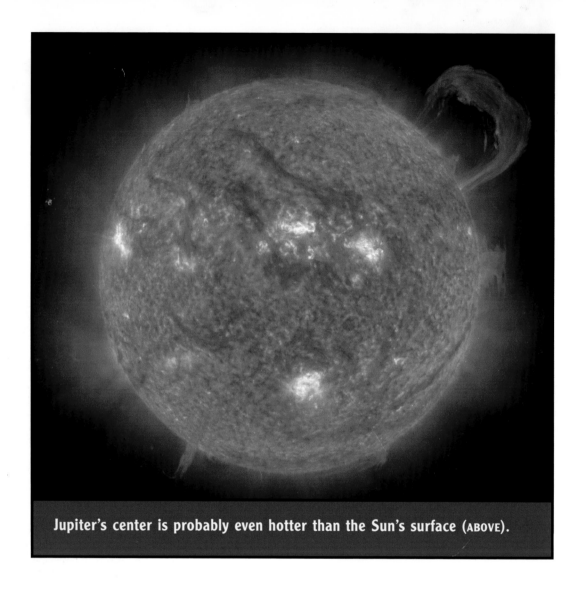

Jupiter's center is probably even hotter than the Sun's surface (ABOVE).

At its center, Jupiter is very hot. Its temperature may be as high as 36,000°F (20,000°C)! That is much hotter than Earth's center.

Jupiter may have a solid core about as large as Earth. This solid core may be made of ice and rock. It is too hot to be frozen. But the core is under extreme pressure. The pressure squeezes the ice and rock into very dense solid material.

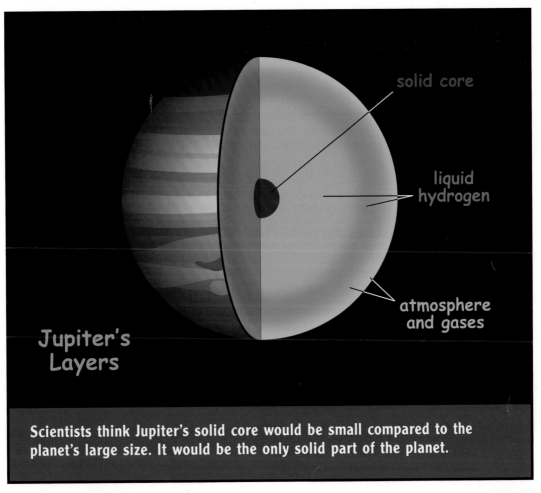

solid core

liquid hydrogen

atmosphere and gases

Jupiter's Layers

Scientists think Jupiter's solid core would be small compared to the planet's large size. It would be the only solid part of the planet.

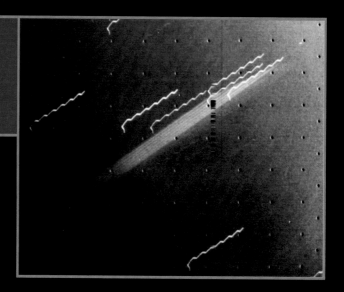

This photo shows part of a faint ring around Jupiter. How did scientists discover something so dark and far from Earth?

CHAPTER 4

JUPITER'S CROWDED NEIGHBORHOOD

Many objects are found in space near Jupiter. A thin ring surrounds Jupiter. This ring is dark and hard to see. It is probably made of bits of dust. No one knew about it until 1979. That year, the spacecraft *Voyager 1* flew by Jupiter. It took a photo that showed the ring. The photo surprised everyone!

Jupiter's ring is made up of three parts. These three parts are the main ring, the halo ring, and the gossamer (GAH-suh-mur) ring. The gossamer ring is the widest. But it is the thinnest from top to bottom and is the hardest to see.

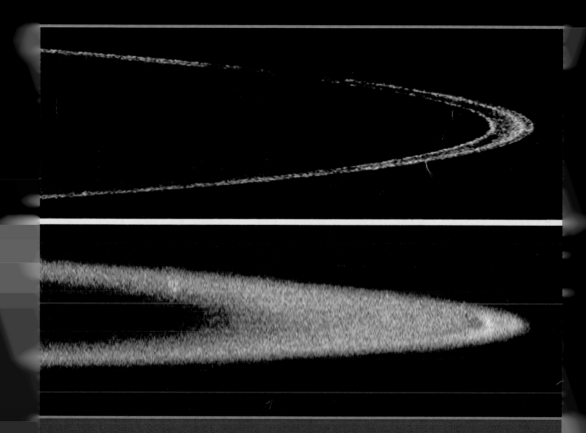

The *New Horizons* spacecraft took these two images of Jupiter's rings in 2007. The top image shows the three parts of the ring as the spacecraft approached the planet. The bottom image was taken as *New Horizons* passed Jupiter and looked back at the planet toward the Sun.

Jupiter also has sixty-three moons that travel around it. Most of these moons are much smaller than Earth's Moon. A few don't even have a name yet. But four of Jupiter's moons are big. They are about the size of Earth's Moon or even bigger. The four big moons are Io, Europa, Ganymede, and Callisto.

Jupiter looms next to its four biggest moons (TOP TO BOTTOM), Io, Europa, Ganymede, and Callisto. Jupiter's Great Red Spot can be seen on the planet.

Jupiter's moon Io has many volcanoes.

Io (EYE-oh) is the big moon closest to
Jupiter. This moon has many volcanoes. The
volcanoes are bubbling and hot. They shoot out
red-hot lava. Io has the most active volcanoes of
anything in our solar system.

Europa (yoo-ROH-pah) is the next closest big moon. It is a little smaller than Earth's Moon. Europa is covered with brown-streaked ice. Scientists think liquid water is below the ice. All living creatures need water. So maybe the water on Europa has living creatures in it! Scientists want to explore Europa more to study its water.

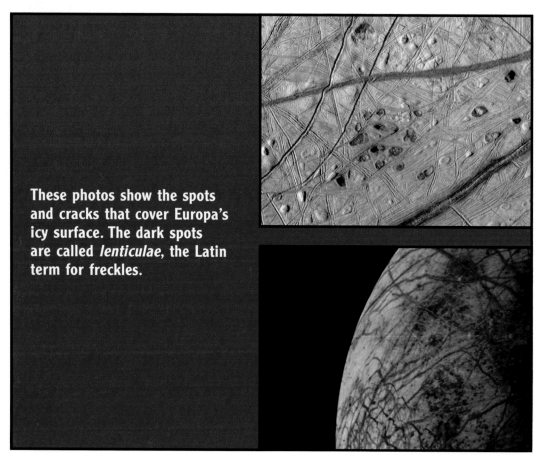

These photos show the spots and cracks that cover Europa's icy surface. The dark spots are called *lenticulae*, the Latin term for freckles.

Jupiter's largest moon, Ganymede, is shown in these images. The surface of Ganymede is rocky and icy.

Ganymede (GAN-ee-meed) is the next big moon out from Jupiter. It is the largest moon in our solar system. This moon is gray, rocky, and icy. It looks a lot like Earth's Moon. Grooves and ridges stretch over the brighter areas of Ganymede.

Callisto (kuh-LIHS-toh) is the last big moon. It is the third-largest moon in the solar system. Callisto has a dark, icy surface. It is covered with bowl-shaped holes called craters. Callisto may have more craters than any other moon.

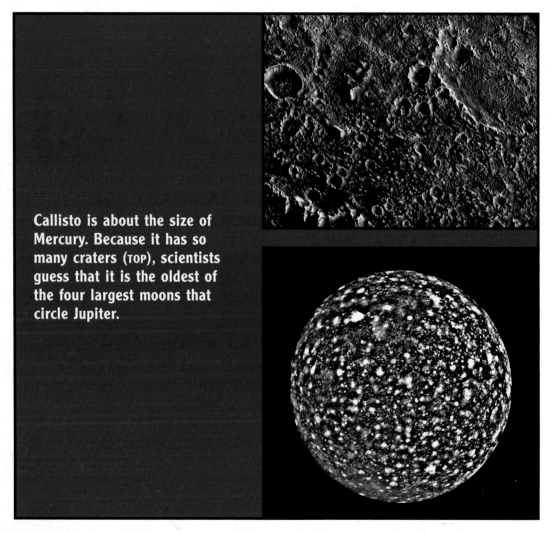

Callisto is about the size of Mercury. Because it has so many craters (TOP), scientists guess that it is the oldest of the four largest moons that circle Jupiter.

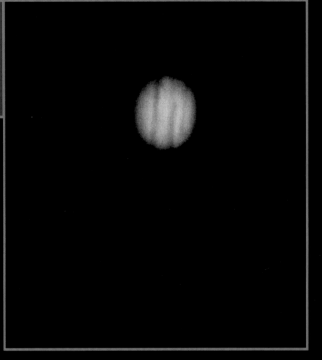

This image of Jupiter shows what the planet looks like through a telescope. Why can't we see Jupiter very well?

CHAPTER 5
EXPLORING JUPITER

Scientists who study space are called astronomers (uh-STRAH-nuh-murz). Until the 1970s, astronomers studied Jupiter with telescopes. They learned as much as they could. But Jupiter is very far away. Even with the best telescopes, scientists couldn't see it closely enough to learn much.

Pioneer 10 was launched in 1969. The spacecraft flew past Jupiter a few years later. It sent back the first close-up images of the planet.

Then, in 1973 and 1974, two spacecraft flew past Jupiter. These spacecraft were named *Pioneer 10* and *Pioneer 11*. The two spacecraft took the first close-up photos of Jupiter and several of its moons. They also found that Jupiter is made mostly of hydrogen.

In 1979, two more spacecraft flew past Jupiter. These were *Voyager 1* and *Voyager 2*. They took better photos than *Pioneer 10* and *11*. Some of these photos showed that Jupiter has a dark ring around it.

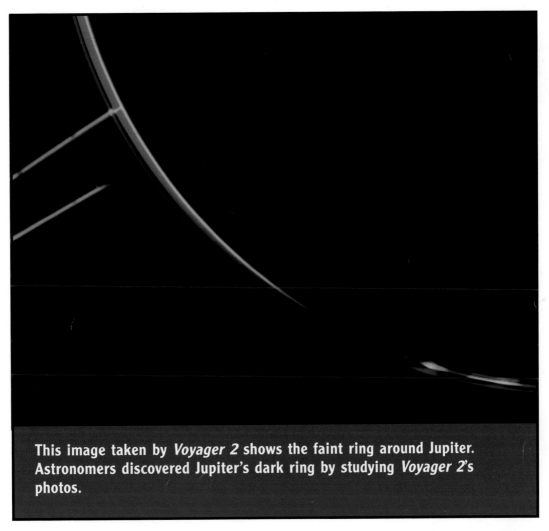

This image taken by *Voyager 2* shows the faint ring around Jupiter. Astronomers discovered Jupiter's dark ring by studying *Voyager 2*'s photos.

Voyager 1 and *2* also sent images of four more moons around Jupiter. And they sent back many photos of Jupiter's four biggest moons. These photos showed Io up close. For the first time, scientists saw Io's hot, bubbling volcanoes!

One of Io's volcanoes explodes in this image from 1979.

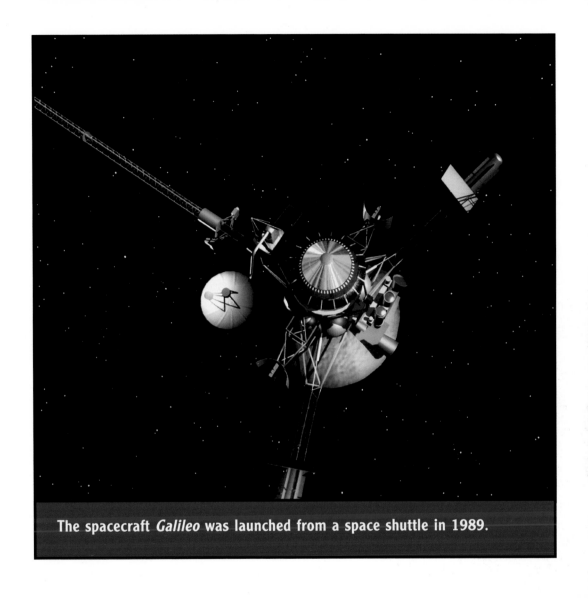

The spacecraft *Galileo* was launched from a space shuttle in 1989.

Galileo was the next spacecraft to fly to
Jupiter. It began to orbit Jupiter in 1995, after a
journey of six years. It took close-up photos of
Jupiter and several moons.

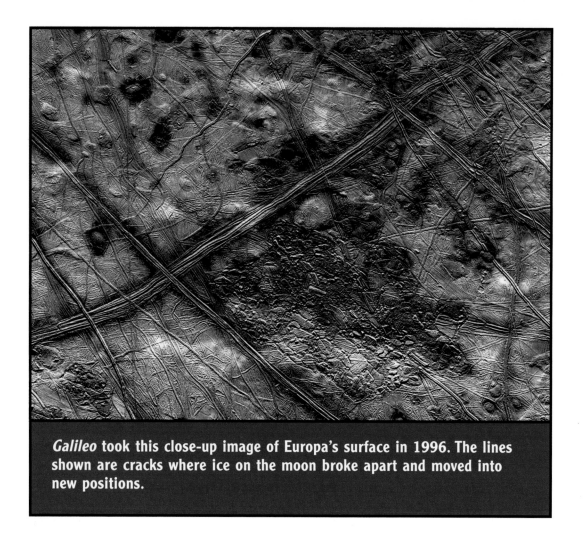

Galileo took this close-up image of Europa's surface in 1996. The lines shown are cracks where ice on the moon broke apart and moved into new positions.

Galileo took close-up photos of Europa in 1996. From these photos, scientists discovered that liquid water probably lies beneath the icy surface. Never before had astronomers found liquid water outside of Earth.

In 2001, *Galileo* found a big new volcano erupting on Io. This volcano blasted lava more than 300 miles (about 500 km) out into space!

Galileo's camera captured this volcanic eruption (RIGHT) on Io's surface (ABOVE).

Galileo also launched a special machine called a probe. This probe flew through Jupiter's clouds and into its atmosphere. For almost an hour, the probe sent back information. The probe found very high wind speeds. It also found hotter and hotter temperatures. Then, after 58 minutes, the probe stopped working. It was melted by the blazing heat inside Jupiter's atmosphere.

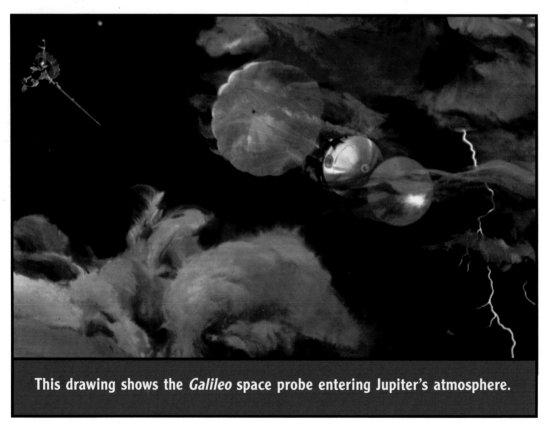

This drawing shows the *Galileo* space probe entering Jupiter's atmosphere.

People on Earth can study Jupiter through a telescope or see it in the night sky.

Astronomers have learned a lot about Jupiter from these spacecraft. But they still have many questions. Perhaps one day you will become an astronomer. If you do, you might help find out more about this interesting planet.

ON SHARING A BOOK

When you share a book with a child, you show that reading is important. To get the most out of the experience, read in a comfortable, quiet place. Turn off the television and limit other distractions, such as telephone calls. Be prepared to start slowly. Take turns reading parts of this book. Stop occasionally and discuss what you're reading. Talk about the photographs. If the child begins to lose interest, stop reading. When you pick up the book again, revisit the parts you have already read.

BE A VOCABULARY DETECTIVE

The word list on page 5 contains words that are important in understanding the topic of this book. Be word detectives and search for the words as you read the book together. Talk about what the words mean and how they are used in the sentence. Do any of these words have more than one meaning? You will find the words defined in a glossary on page 46.

WHAT ABOUT QUESTIONS?

Use questions to make sure the child understands the information in this book. Here are some suggestions:

> What did this paragraph tell us? What does this picture show? What do you think we'll learn about next? Which planets are between Jupiter and the Sun? What are the names of Jupiter's four biggest moons? What is your favorite part of the book? Why?

If the child has questions, don't hesitate to respond with questions of your own, such as What do *you* think? Why? What is it that you don't know? If the child can't remember certain facts, turn to the index.

INTRODUCING THE INDEX

The index helps readers find information without searching through the whole book. Turn to the index on page 48. Choose an entry such as *telescope,* and ask the child to use the index to find out how telescopes help astronomers. Repeat with as many entries as you like. Ask the child to point out the differences between an index and a glossary. (The index helps readers find information, while the glossary tells readers what words mean.)

JUPITER

BOOKS

Asimov, Isaac. *Astronomy in Ancient Times*. Milwaukee: Gareth Stevens, 2006. Learn how people studied stars and planets such as Jupiter before modern science equipment was invented.

Hansen, Rosanna. *Mysteries in Space: A Chapter Book*. New York: Children's Press, 2005. This book describes a few of the many mysteries found in space, beginning with a huge fireball.

Hansen, Rosanna. *Space: A Chapter Book*. New York: Children's Press, 2003. Find out about the first moon landing, how astronauts live and work in space, and what lies beyond our solar system.

Simon, Seymour. *Our Solar System*. Updated ed. New York: Collins, 2007. This overview of the solar system features vivid photos and colorful illustrations.

WEBSITES

ESA—Kids
http://www.esa.int/esaKIDSen/index.html
This European Space Agency site is packed with activities, photos, and space news. Find out how space technology has helped us on Earth!

Jupiter: Kid's Eye View
http://solarsystem.nasa.gov/planets/profile.cfm?Object=Jupiter&Display=Kids
Find out how much you would weigh on Jupiter! This NASA website also has facts and figures and links to help you learn more.

NASA Kids' Club
http://www.nasa.gov/audience/forkids/kidsclub/flash/index.html
Check out current space missions, games, and tons of photos.

The Space Place
http://spaceplace.nasa.gov/en/kids/
This NASA site features activities, quizzes, and games all about space.

GLOSSARY

astronomer (uh-STRAH-nuh-mur): a scientist who studies outer space

atmosphere (AT-muhs-feer): a blanket of gases that surrounds a planet

axis (AK-sihs): an imaginary line that runs through the center of an object such as a planet. A planet spins around its axis.

crater: a bowl-shaped hole in the surface of a planet or moon

gas giant: a planet that is made up mostly of gases

Kuiper belt (KY-pur-behlt): a region of outer space beyond Neptune that is filled with rocks, ice, and dwarf planets, including Pluto

orbit: a curved path around an object in space, such as the Sun or a planet. To orbit can also mean to move along this path.

rotate (ROH-tayt): to spin on an axis

solar system: the group of objects in space that includes the Sun, the planets, their moons, and other objects

spacecraft: a vehicle that travels in space

telescope (TEH-luh-skohp): an instrument that makes distant objects look closer. Scientists use telescopes to learn more about space.

INDEX

Pages listed in **bold** type refer to images.